Great Works Instructional Guides for Literature

The Fire Cat

Based on the book by Esther Averill
Great Works Author: Debra J. Housel

SHELL EDUCATION

Image Credits

John Nez (cover, p. 1, p. 11, p. 36); Timothy J. Bradley (p. 12, p. 44); Shutterstock (p. 14, p. 24, p. 25, p. 34, p. 47, p. 53, p. 56)

Standards

© 2007 Teachers of English to Speakers of Other Languages, Inc. (TESOL)
© 2007 Board of Regents of the University of Wisconsin System. World-Class Instructional Design and Assessment (WIDA)
© Copyright 2010. National Governors Association Center for Best Practices and Council of Chief State School Officers. All rights reserved.

Shell Education

5301 Oceanus Drive
Huntington Beach, CA 92649-1030
http://www.shelleducation.com

ISBN 978-1-4807-6911-3

© 2015 Shell Educational Publishing, Inc.

Table of Contents

How to Use This Literature Guide

Today's standards demand rigor and relevance in the reading of complex texts. The units in this series guide teachers in a rich and deep exploration of worthwhile works of literature for classroom study. The most rigorous instruction can also be interesting and engaging!

Many current strategies for effective literacy instruction have been incorporated into these instructional guides for literature. Throughout the units, text-dependent questions are used to determine comprehension of the book as well as student interpretation of the vocabulary words. The books chosen for the series are complex and are exemplars of carefully crafted works of literature. Close reading is used throughout the units to guide students toward revisiting the text and using textual evidence to respond to prompts orally and in writing. Students must analyze the story elements in multiple assignments for each section of the book. All of these strategies work together to rigorously guide students through their study of literature.

The next few pages describe how to use this guide for a purposeful and meaningful literature study. Each section of this guide is set up in the same way to make it easier for you to implement the instruction in your classroom.

Theme Thoughts

The great works of literature used throughout this series have important themes that have been relevant to people for many years. Many of the themes will be discussed during the various sections of this instructional guide. However, it would also benefit students to have independent time to think about the key themes of the book.

Before students begin reading, have them complete the *Pre-Reading Theme Thoughts* (page 13). This graphic organizer will allow students to think about the themes outside the context of the story. They'll have the opportunity to evaluate statements based on important themes and defend their opinions. Be sure to keep students' papers for comparison to the *Post-Reading Theme Thoughts* (page 58). This graphic organizer is similar to the pre-reading activity. However, this time, students will be answering the questions from the point of view of one of the characters in the book. They have to think about how the character would feel about each statement and defend their thoughts. To conclude the activity, have students compare what they thought about the themes before they read the book to what the characters discovered during the story.

Pre-Reading Picture Walks

For each section in this literature guide, there are suggestions for how to introduce the text to students. Teachers share information in a visual format and ask students to evaluate the content. Students must use the information presented in the illustrations to discuss what they are about to read and make predictions about the sections.

How to Use This Literature Guide *(cont.)*

Vocabulary

Each teacher reference vocabulary overview page has definitions and sentences about how key vocabulary words are used in the section. These words should be introduced and discussed with students. Students will use these words in different activities throughout the book.

On some of the vocabulary student pages, students are asked to answer text-related questions about vocabulary words from the sections. The following question stems will help you create your own vocabulary questions if you'd like to extend the discussion.

- How does this word describe _____'s character?
- How does this word connect to the problem in this story?
- How does this word help you understand the setting?
- Tell me how this word connects to the main idea of this story.
- What visual pictures does this word bring to your mind?
- Why do you think the author used this word?

At times, you may find that more work with the words will help students understand their meanings and importance. These quick vocabulary activities are a good way to further study the words.

- Students can play vocabulary concentration. Make one set of cards that has the words on them and another set with the definitions. Then, have students lay them out on the table and play concentration. The goal of the game is to match vocabulary words with their definitions. For early readers or English language learners, the two sets of cards could be the words and pictures of the words.

- Students can create word journal entries about the words. Students choose words they think are important and then describe why they think each word is important within the book. Early readers or English language learners could instead draw pictures about the words in a journal.

- Students can create puppets and use them to act out the vocabulary words from the stories. Students may also enjoy telling their own character-driven stories using vocabulary words from the original stories.

How to Use This Literature Guide (cont.)

Analyzing the Literature

After you have read each section with students, hold a small-group or whole-class discussion. Provided on the teacher reference page for each section are leveled questions. The questions are written at two levels of complexity to allow you to decide which questions best meet the needs of your students. The Level 1 questions are typically less abstract than the Level 2 questions. These questions are focused on the various story elements, such as character, setting, and plot. Be sure to add further questions as your students discuss what they've read. For each question, a few key points are provided for your reference as you discuss the book with students.

Reader Response

In today's classrooms, there are often great readers who are below average writers. So much time and energy is spent in classrooms getting students to read on grade level that little time is left to focus on writing skills. To help teachers include more writing in their daily literacy instruction, each section of this guide has a literature-based reader response prompt. Each of the three genres of writing is used in the reader responses within this guide: narrative, informative/explanatory, and opinion. Before students write, you may want to allow them time to draw pictures related to the topic.

Guided Close Reading

Within each section of this guide, it is suggested that you closely reread a portion of the text with your students. Page numbers are given, but since some versions of the books may have different page numbers, the sections to be reread are described by location as well. After rereading the section, there are a few text-dependent questions to be answered by students.

Working space has been provided to help students prepare for the group discussion. They should record their thoughts and ideas on the activity page and refer to it during your discussion. Rather than just taking notes, you may want to require students to write complete responses to the questions before discussing them with you.

Encourage students to read one question at a time and then go back to the text and discover the answer. Work with students to ensure that they use the text to determine their answers rather than making unsupported inferences. Suggested answers are provided in the answer key.

How to Use This Literature Guide (cont.)

Guided Close Reading (cont.)

The generic open-ended stems below can be used to write your own text-dependent questions if you would like to give students more practice.

- What words in the story support . . . ?
- What text helps you understand . . . ?
- Use the book to tell why _____ happens.
- Based on the events in the story, . . . ?
- Show me the part in the text that supports . . . .
- Use the text to tell why . . . .

Making Connections

The activities in this section help students make cross-curricular connections to mathematics, science, social studies, fine arts, or other curricular areas. These activities require higher-order thinking skills from students but also allow for creative thinking.

Language Learning

A special section has been set aside to connect the literature to language conventions. Through these activities, students will have opportunities to practice the conventions of standard English grammar, usage, capitalization, and punctuation.

Story Elements

It is important to spend time discussing what the common story elements are in literature. Understanding the characters, setting, plot, and theme can increase students' comprehension and appreciation of the story. If teachers begin discussing these elements in early childhood, students will more likely internalize the concepts and look for the elements in their independent reading. Another very important reason for focusing on the story elements is that students will be better writers if they think about how the stories they read are constructed.

In the story elements activities, students are asked to create work related to the characters, setting, or plot. Consider having students complete only one of these activities. If you give students a choice on this assignment, each student can decide to complete the activity that most appeals to him or her. Different intelligences are used so that the activities are diverse and interesting to all students.

How to Use This Literature Guide (cont.)

Culminating Activity

At the end of this instructional guide is a creative culminating activity that allows students the opportunity to share what they've learned from reading the book. This activity is open ended so that students can push themselves to create their own great works within your language arts classroom.

Comprehension Assessment

The questions in this section require students to think about the book they've read as well as the words that were used in the book. Some questions are tied to quotations from the book to engage students and require them to think about the text as they answer the questions.

Response to Literature

Finally, students are asked to respond to the literature by drawing pictures and writing about the characters and stories. A suggested rubric is provided for teacher reference.

Correlation to the Standards

Shell Education is committed to producing educational materials that are research and standards based. As part of this effort, we have correlated all of our products to the academic standards of all 50 states, the District of Columbia, the Department of Defense Dependents Schools, and all Canadian provinces.

Purpose and Intent of Standards

Standards are designed to focus instruction and guide adoption of curricula. Standards are statements that describe the criteria necessary for students to meet specific academic goals. They define the knowledge, skills, and content students should acquire at each level. Standards are also used to develop standardized tests to evaluate students' academic progress. Teachers are required to demonstrate how their lessons meet standards. Standards are used in the development of all of our products, so educators can be assured they meet high academic standards.

How to Find Standards Correlations

To print a customized correlation report of this product for your state, visit our website at http://www.shelleducation.com and follow the online directions. If you require assistance in printing correlation reports, please contact our Customer Service Department at 1-877-777-3450.

Correlation to the Standards (cont.)

Standards Correlation Chart

The lessons in this book were written to support the Common Core College and Career Readiness Anchor Standards. The following chart indicates which lessons address the anchor standards.

Common Core College and Career Readiness Anchor Standard	Section
CCSS.ELA-Literacy.CCRA.R.1—Read closely to determine what the text says explicitly and to make logical inferences from it; cite specific textual evidence when writing or speaking to support conclusions drawn from the text.	Guided Close Reading Sections 1–4; Analyzing the Literature Sections 1–4; Making Connections Section 3; Story Elements Sections 2–4
CCSS.ELA-Literacy.CCRA.R.2—Determine central ideas or themes of a text and analyze their development; summarize the key supporting details and ideas.	Story Elements Section 3; Making Connections Sections 1–2
CCSS.ELA-Literacy.CCRA.R.3—Analyze how and why individuals, events, or ideas develop and interact over the course of a text.	Analyzing the Literature Sections 1–4; Story Elements Sections 1, 3
CCSS.ELA-Literacy.CCRA.R.4—Interpret words and phrases as they are used in a text, including determining technical, connotative, and figurative meanings, and analyze how specific word choices shape meaning or tone.	Vocabulary Sections 1–4
CCSS.ELA-Literacy.CCRA.R.5—Analyze the structure of texts, including how specific sentences, paragraphs, and larger portions of the text (e.g., a section, chapter, scene, or stanza) relate to each other and the whole.	Guided Close Reading Sections 1–4
CCSS.ELA-Literacy.CCRA.R.6—Assess how point of view or purpose shapes the content and style of a text.	Story Elements Section 2; Post-Reading Theme Thoughts
CCSS.ELA-Literacy.CCRA.R.7—Integrate and evaluate content presented in diverse media and formats, including visually and quantitatively, as well as in words.	Pre-Reading Picture Walk Sections 1–4; Story Elements Section 3
CCSS.ELA-Literacy.CCRA.R.10—Read and comprehend complex literary and informational texts independently and proficiently.	Entire Unit
CCSS.ELA-Literacy.CCRA.W.1—Write arguments to support claims in an analysis of substantive topics or texts using valid reasoning and relevant and sufficient evidence.	Reader Response Section 4; Story Elements Section 4; Post-Reading Response to Literature
CCSS.ELA-Literacy.CCRA.W.2—Write informative/explanatory texts to examine and convey complex ideas and information clearly and accurately through the effective selection, organization, and analysis of content.	Reader Response Section 3; Post Reading Response to Literature
CCSS.ELA-Literacy.CCRA.W.3—Write narratives to develop real or imagined experiences or events using effective technique, well-chosen details and well-structured event sequences.	Reader Response Sections 1–2; Making Connections Section 1; Post-Reading Response to Literature

Common Core College and Career Readiness Anchor Standard	Section
CCSS.ELA-Literacy.CCRA.W.4—Produce clear and coherent writing in which the development, organization, and style are appropriate to task, purpose, and audience.	Reader Response Sections 1–4; Making Connections Section 1; Post-Reading Response to Literature
CCSS.ELA-Literacy.CCRA.W.9—Draw evidence from literary or informational texts to support analysis, reflection, and research.	Making Connections Section 3
CCSS.ELA-Literacy.CCRA.W.10—Write routinely over extended time frames (time for research, reflection, and revision) and shorter time frames (a single sitting or a day or two) for a range of tasks, purposes, and audiences.	Reader Response Sections 1–4; Post-Reading Response to Literature
CCSS.ELA-Literacy.CCRA.SL.1—Prepare for and participate effectively in a range of conversations and collaborations with diverse partners, building on others' ideas and expressing their own clearly and persuasively.	Analyzing the Literature Sections 1–4; Guided Close Reading Sections 1–4
CCSS.ELA-Literacy.CCRA.L.1—Demonstrate command of the conventions of standard English grammar and usage when writing or speaking.	Language Learning Sections 1–4; Reader Response Sections 1–4; Post-Reading Response to Literature
CCSS.ELA-Literacy.CCRA.L.2—Demonstrate command of the conventions of standard English capitalization, punctuation, and spelling when writing.	Reader Response Sections 1–4; Post-Reading Response to Literature
CCSS.ELA-Literacy.CCRA.L.3—Apply knowledge of language to understand how language functions in different contexts, to make effective choices for meaning or style, and to comprehend more fully when reading or listening.	Vocabulary Sections 1–4; Language Learning Sections 1–4
CCSS.ELA-Literacy.CCRA.L.6—Acquire and use accurately a range of general academic and domain-specific words and phrases sufficient for reading, writing, speaking, and listening at the college and career readiness level; demonstrate independence in gathering vocabulary knowledge when encountering an unknown term important to comprehension or expression.	Vocabulary Sections 1–4

TESOL and WIDA Standards

The lessons in this book promote English language development for English language learners. The following TESOL and WIDA English Language Development Standards are addressed through the activities in this book:

- **Standard 1:** English language learners communicate for social and instructional purposes within the school setting.

- **Standard 2:** English language learners communicate information, ideas and concepts necessary for academic success in the content area of language arts.

About the Author—Esther Averill

Esther Averill was born in 1902 in Bridgeport, Connecticut. As a teenager, she drew cartoons for a local newspaper. In 1925, she graduated from Vassar College and moved to Paris, France. She then worked as a photojournalist's assistant. While in France, she wrote a few children's picture books and started Domino Press, a children's book imprint. Domino Press struggled and eventually shut down after seven years.

Averill returned to the United States in 1941 and worked in the New York Public Library. In 1944, she wrote and illustrated a book entitled *The Cat Club*. It was the first of 13 stories about Jenny Linsky, a black cat who wears a red scarf and lives with Captain Tinker in New York City. In 1960, Miss Averill stepped away from the Jenny stories long enough to write and illustrate *The Fire Cat*, which became one of her most popular books. Each of the cats in her books is based on a cat she actually owned or knew. Averill died in 1992.

Possible Texts for Text Comparisons

Esther Averill wrote 13 other cat stories, most of them starring Jenny Linsky. These titles are in print: *Jenny and the Cat Club*, *The School for Cats*, *Jenny's Birthday Book*, *Jenny Goes to Sea*, *Jenny's Moonlight Adventure*, *The Hotel Cat*, and *Captains of the City Streets*.

Cross-Curricular Connection

This book can be used in a unit on fire safety, making friends, and/or bullying. More resources and webisodes on bullying are available from: **http://www.stopbullying.gov/kids/webisodes/**.

Book Summary of *The Fire Cat*

Pickles is a homeless cat with big paws who lives in a barrel. He longs to do something "big" but doesn't know what that something is. Instead, he entertains himself by bullying smaller cats and chasing them away whenever they venture into his area.

Mrs. Goodkind loves cats and has several of her own. She watches Pickles from her window and takes him food each day. One day she decides to bring him into her home. But Pickles doesn't want to sit in a pretty chair or play with toys. He goes back to his barrel. One day he chases a little cat up a tree and refuses to let her climb down. The wind blows and then rain falls, so Pickles finally lets the other cat go. But then Pickles can't get down! Mrs. Goodkind calls the firehouse. A fire truck comes, and a firefighter named Joe rescues Pickles.

Joe takes the cat back to the firehouse. No one knows if the chief will allow Pickles to stay. So Pickles sets about learning to be a firefighter. He learns how to slide down the pole. He learns how to jump up in the fire truck and ride along. He helps to hold a hose steady at a fire. The chief presents Pickles with his very own tiny fire hat. He is officially a fire cat!

Pickles has won over the firefighters, but he still doesn't get along with other cats. In fact, he chases away any that come to the firehouse. The chief tells him that he must be kind to other cats. Over time, Pickles learns to enjoy having other cats hang around the firehouse. One day, Pickles rides on the fire truck to the very tree where he had been stuck. One of Mrs. Goodkind's smallest cat is high up in the small branches where a human cannot go. Pickles bravely climbs the ladder, goes to the high branch, picks up the cat by the scruff of its neck, and carries it gently to the ground. Mrs. Goodkind praises him and says that he has done something very big. Pickles is now a proud, happy cat who knows that this is just the start of his doing big things.

Possible Texts for Text Sets

- Bruel, Nick. *Bad Kitty*. Square Fish, 2005. (This is the first of many titles in a *New York Times* best-selling series.)

- Dean, James. *Pete the Cat*. HarperCollins, 2010. (This is the first title in a popular series.)

- Hayward, Linda. *Jobs People Do—A Day in a Life of a Firefighter*. DK Children, 2001.

- Liebman, Dan. *I Want to Be a Firefighter*. Firefly Books, 1999.

Pre-Reading Theme Thoughts

Directions: For each statement, draw a picture of a happy face or a sad face. Your face should show how you feel about the statement. Then, use words to say why you feel that way.

Statement	How Do You Feel? ☺ ☹	Explain Your Answer
I feel like I don't belong.		
I want to do something important.		
I work hard to show others I can do it.		
I like to help people in need.		

Pre-Reading Picture Walk

1. Show students the front cover of the book. Ask them to identify the title and the author for the story. Explain that since no illustrator is mentioned that it means the author also drew the pictures for the book.

2. Explain that good readers make predictions before reading. A prediction is making a guess about characters or what will happen in a story. One way to do this is to examine the pictures before reading.

3. Ask students to identify the main character on the cover. (*Fire cat is on the cover. His name also appears in the title.*) Based on the front cover illustration, ask, "What is the fire cat doing?" (*He is wearing a fire hat and sliding down a pole.*)

4. Turn to page 3. Explain that this book has chapters. Each chapter is listed in the Table of Contents. Ask different students to identify the name of the third chapter, the first chapter, and the second chapter. As each student identifies the name of the chapter, ask what page each chapter begins on.

5. Turn to page 5. Cover the text. Have students describe what the cat looks like. (*He has yellow fur with black spots.*) Based on the next two pictures, what else can they infer about the cat.

General Note: The book is more than 50 years old and thus shows the possessive of Pickles as Pickles'. The rule is now to show possessive of proper nouns that end in –s with an apostrophe s. We want to encourage kids to write it correctly, so this instructional guide will show the possessive as Pickles's.

Vocabulary Overview

Key words and phrases from this section are provided below with definitions and sentences about how the words are used in the story. Introduce and discuss these important vocabulary words with students. If you think these words or other words in the story warrant more time devoted to them, there are suggestions in the introduction for other vocabulary activities (page 5).

Word	Definition	Sentence about Text
anything (p. 6)	a thing of any kind	Pickles can't find **anything** big to do.
barrel (p. 7)	a round, wooden container with curved sides and a flat bottom used for storing things	Pickles lives in a **barrel**.
nothing (p. 8)	not a thing	Since Pickles has **nothing** to do, he chases cats.
something (p. 12)	a thing that is not known, named, or specified	Mrs. Goodkind believes **something** will change for Pickles.
mixed-up (p. 13)	confused; hard to understand	Mrs. Goodkind says that Pickles is a **mixed-up** cat.
happen (p. 17)	occur; to take place usually without planning	Mrs. Goodkind wants good things to **happen** for Pickles.

Name _____ Date _____

Vocabulary Activity

Directions: Draw lines to complete the sentences.

Sentence Beginnings

Each day Mrs. Goodkind

Pickles does not have

The empty **barrel**

What will **happen**

Pickles is both good and bad

Sentence Endings

has **nothing** inside it.

because he is a **mixed-up** cat.

gives Pickles **something** to eat.

anything useful to do.

when a cat comes near Pickles?

Directions: Answer this question.

1. What **happens** when Pickles chases away all the other cats?

_____

_____

Analyzing the Literature

Provided below are discussion questions you can use in small groups, with the whole class, or for written assignments. Each question is written at two levels so you can choose the right question for each group of students. For each question, a few key points are provided for your reference as you discuss the book with students.

Story Element	Level 1	Level 2	Key Discussion Points
Setting	Where does Mrs. Goodkind live?	How does Mrs. Goodkind discover Pickles?	Mrs. Goodkind lives in a house near Pickles's barrel. We know this because her cats look out the window at Pickles.
Plot	How does Pickles get food?	How does Pickles survive living in the old barrel?	Mrs. Goodkind brings him food each day.
Character	How does Pickles feel about other cats?	How do you think other cats feel about Pickles?	Pickles does not get along with other cats. Instead, he chases them. Mrs. Goodkind's cats tell him that he can't be their friend.
Character	Why is the woman named Mrs. Goodkind?	What is the significance of the woman's name?	Mrs. Goodkind is good and kind, so her name lets the reader know right away what her behavior will be.

Name _____ Date _____

Reader Response

Think

Mrs. Goodkind's cats call out to Pickles that he is a bad cat and he can't be their friend. Has anyone ever refused to be your friend?

Narrative Writing Prompt

How would you feel if someone said to you, "You can't be my friend"? Write a journal entry describing your feelings.

Dear Journal,

_____

_____

_____

_____

_____

_____

_____

_____

Guided Close Reading

Closely reread the part where we learn about Mrs. Goodkind's friendship with Pickles (pages 12–15).

Directions: Think about these questions. In the space below, write ideas or draw pictures as you think. Be ready to share your answers.

❶ Use the text to describe what Mrs. Goodkind does for Pickles.

❷ According to the book, why does Mrs. Goodkind call Pickles a mixed-up cat?

❸ Does Mrs. Goodkind's home look like a good place for Pickles to live? Support your answer with details from the text.

Name _____ **Date** _____

Making Connections–Making Friends

Pickles is lonely and bored. He is not helping himself by chasing away all the other cats. Pickles needs to learn how to make friends! Think about how you make friends. What do you do?

Directions: Write an email message to Pickles. Give him advice on how to make friends with the cats that come into his yard.

From: _____

To: _____

Subject: _____

Making Connections-Dreaming Big

Directions: Pickles dreams of doing something big. But he doesn't know what that big thing is. Think about a dream you have. It can be something you want to do, someone you want to meet, or something you'd like to own. Draw a picture of your dream. Then, write a description to tell about it.

_____

_____

_____

_____

Name _____ Date _____

Language Learning–Spelling

Directions: Read these words from the story. Write just the adjectives inside the frame. Use styles and colors to help show what the words mean. For example, you can write the word *yellow* in yellow crayon.

Language Hints!

- An adjective is a describing word.

- Adjectives often tell size, color, or age.

- An adjective helps us to picture a person, place, or thing in our minds.

Words from the Story

yellow	big	black	spots	young	bad	friend
cat	barrel	old	yard	little	house	good

Adjectives

Story Elements–Character

Directions: Fill in the Venn diagram below to compare and contrast Mrs. Goodkind's cats with Pickles. Include at least two or three items in each section of the Venn diagram.

Pickles   **Mrs. Goodkind's Cats**

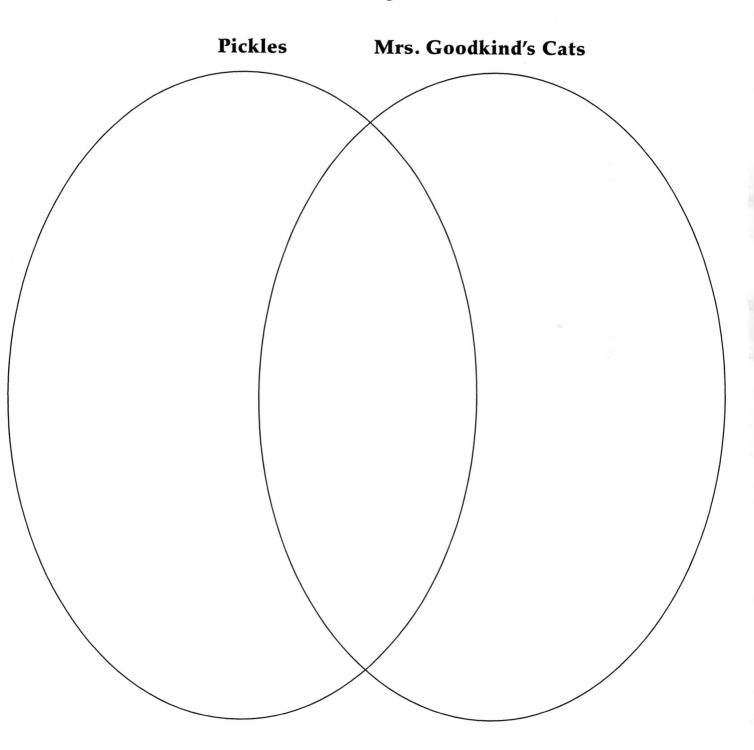

Name _____ Date _____

Story Elements-Setting

Directions: Page 8 shows the setting. Think about where Pickles lives. Then, circle the pictures of things in the environment that could be a danger to him.

Pre-Reading Picture Walk

1. Turn to page 18. Cover the text. Ask students to say what they think is happening in the picture. *(Pickles is following/chasing a smaller cat up a tree.)*

2. Turn to page 21. Have students identify who is at the base of the tree. *(Mrs. Goodkind)* What can we tell about the weather from her? *(It must be raining because she's under an umbrella.)* Where is Pickles? *(still in the tree)* Where is the other cat? *(It must have left the tree.)*

3. Look at the next few pictures slowly. On page 25, have students explain how this illustration differs from the ones that have come before. *(It is showing the picture from Pickles's viewpoint looking down the tree.)* What is the firefighter doing? *(He is climbing a ladder that is against the tree.)* Why is he doing this? *(to save Pickles)*

General Note: The term *fireman* is used throughout the book. In this guide, the term *firefighter* has been used instead. You may want to discuss this word and how its use has changed since this book was first published in 1960. (See page 42 for an activity related to this.)

Vocabulary Overview

Key words and phrases from this section are provided below with definitions and sentences about how the words are used in the story. Introduce and discuss these important vocabulary words with students. If you think these words or other words in the story warrant more time devoted to them, there are suggestions in the introduction for other vocabulary activities (page 5).

Word	Definition	Sentence about Text
climbed (p. 18)	moved up something using one's limbs	Pickles **climbs** the tree.
harder (p. 20)	in a very forceful way	The rain falls **harder** and harder.
sometimes (p. 20)	occasionally	**Sometimes** a cat can't get down from a tree.
telephone (p. 22)	a device used to listen to and speak to someone who is someplace else	Mrs. Goodkind uses the **telephone** to report the problem.
firemen (p. 22)	men who work to put out fires	The **firemen** come to rescue Pickles.
pointed (p. 24)	used a finger to direct attention toward a person or a thing	Mrs. Goodkind **points** to the top of the tree.
ladder (p. 24)	a device used for climbing that has two long pieces of wood, with a series of steps between them	Joe goes up the **ladder** to get Pickles.
tucked (p. 26)	put something in a particular place to keep it safe	Joe **tucks** Pickles inside his coat.
firehouse (p. 31)	the building that holds the members of a fire department and the equipment used to put out fires	Pickles rides on the fire truck to the **firehouse**.

Pickles Up a Tree

Vocabulary Activity

Directions: Choose at least two words from the story. Draw a picture that shows what these words mean. Label your picture.

Words from the Story

climbed	telephone	firemen	pointed	ladder	firehouse

Directions: Answer the question.

1. Why does Mrs. Goodkind use the **telephone**?

_____

_____

Analyzing the Literature

Provided below are discussion questions you can use in small groups, with the whole class, or for written assignments. Each question is written at two levels so you can choose the right question for each group of students. For each question, a few key points are provided for your reference as you discuss the book with students.

Story Element	Level 1	Level 2	Key Discussion Points
Character	Name at least two of Mrs. Goodkind's traits.	What do we know about Mrs. Goodkind's personality?	Mrs. Goodkind is nice and caring. She clearly cares about cats and goes out of her way to make sure that Pickles gets rescued. She wants Pickles to be happy.
Plot	Why does Pickles chase the cat up the tree?	Why does Pickles chase cats away from his barrel?	Pickles is a bully. He chases every cat he sees. He follows the cat up the tree to prevent her from getting down.
Character	How does Pickles feel when he gets stuck in the tree?	What does Pickles think when Mrs. Goodkind urges him to get down?	Pickles feels frightened because he is high up in the tree during a storm. When Mrs. Goodkind calls to him, he realizes that he is unable to save himself.
Setting	How does Mrs. Goodkind find out that Pickles is in trouble?	Why is it important to the story that Mrs. Goodkind's house is close to the tree?	Mrs. Goodkind's house is close to the tree, so she sees him stuck up there during the storm. It's important to the story that her house is nearby because otherwise she wouldn't have found him.

Reader Response

Think

Think of a time when you helped someone else. Or, think of a time when someone helped you.

Narrative Writing Prompt

Describe a time when you helped another person. If you prefer, write about a time when someone helped you.

_____

_____

_____

_____

_____

_____

_____

_____

_____

_____

Name _____ Date _____

Guided Close Reading

Closely reread about what happens in the tree on page 20.

Directions: Think about these questions. In the space below, write ideas or draw pictures as you think. Be ready to share your answers.

❶ What words in the text describe the weather?

❷ Based on the events in the story, how does Pickles treat the little cat?

❸ Use the text to tell how we know that Pickles cannot save himself.

Making Connections—Don't Be a Bully!

Directions: Pickles is a bully. He is mean to the little cat. Being a bully is wrong. Read each caption. Draw a picture to match it.

Do not do or say anything to hurt someone.

If you feel like being mean, walk away. Do something else.

Each person is different. Not good or bad—just different.

If you have been mean to someone, say you are sorry.

Name _____ Date _____

Making Connections–Calling 9-1-1

Directions: Mrs. Goodkind calls for help when Pickles gets stuck. In an emergency, you should call 9-1-1. The operator will send police officers, firefighters, or an ambulance to help you. Make a list of emergencies where you might have to call 9-1-1.

- *a car accident*

- _____

- _____

- _____

- _____

- _____

- _____

- _____

- _____

- _____

Language Learning–Nouns

Directions: Read the words from the chapter. Some are proper nouns and the rest are nouns. Write each word in the appropriate box below.

Language Hints!

- A noun is a person, place, or thing.

- A proper noun is the specific name of a person or place.

Words from the Book

Pickles	cat	tree	Mrs. Goodkind
rain	barrel	window	firemen
Joe	ladder	coat	wind

Nouns	**Proper Nouns**

Story Elements–Character

Directions: Pickles chases the little cat up the tree. Write about this event from the little cat's point of view.

_____

_____

_____

_____

_____

_____

_____

_____

_____

_____

_____

Story Elements-Plot

Directions: Create a list of the five main events that happened in this part of the story. Cut out each event. Then, give the events to a friend to put in order of how they happened. Check your friend's work.

Pre-Reading Picture Walk

1. Turn to page 3, which has the Table of Contents. Remind students that this book has chapters. Ask students to identify the name of the second chapter and the page number on which it begins. *("The Fire Cat"; page 32)*

2. Turn to pages 32–33. Cover the text. Ask, "What is the setting for this chapter?" *(a fire station named Hook & Ladder Company 7)*

3. Turn to page 39. Ask, "What are the men doing?" *(sliding down a pole in the fire station)*

4. Turn to page 43. Ask, "What is happening?" *(Pickles is sliding down the pole.)*

5. Turn to page 47. Ask, "What is Joe doing here?" *(spraying water on a fire)* What is Pickles doing to help him? *(He is holding the hose.)*

6. Turn to page 49. Ask, "Who is in the picture?" *(Pickles, Mrs. Goodkind, and the firefighters in their uniforms)*

General Note: The book treats the word *chief* as a proper noun, always capitalizing it even though it's not followed by a surname. In this guide, we chose to follow the grammatical convention of not capitalizing this title.

Vocabulary Overview

Key words and phrases from this section are provided below with definitions and sentences about how the words are used in the story. Introduce and discuss these important vocabulary words with students. If you think these words or other words in the story warrant more time devoted to them, there are suggestions in the introduction for other vocabulary activities (page 5).

Word	Definition	Sentence about Text
chief (p. 32)	the person who leads a group of people	The **chief** says he will think about letting Pickles stay.
answered (p. 34)	responded to something or someone	The chief **answers** the phone and talks to Mrs. Goodkind.
quietly (p. 36)	to do while making very little noise	Pickles follows Joe **quietly** up the stairs in the firehouse.
suddenly (p. 38)	done in an unexpected way	The fire bell rings **suddenly**.
slide (p. 40)	to move smoothly; to glide	Pickles practices how to **slide** down the pole.
learning (p. 44)	the process of gaining knowledge or skill	**Learning** to slide down the pole takes time.
everything (p. 44)	all the things in a group	Pickles wants to learn to do **everything** the firefighters can do.
straight (p. 45)	having no curves, bends, or angles	The fire cat sits up **straight** while riding on the fire truck.

Name _____ Date _____

Vocabulary Activity

Directions: Practice your writing skills. Write at least two sentences using words from the story.

Words from the Story

chief	straight	quietly	slide	everything

_____

_____

_____

_____

_____

_____

_____

Directions: Answer this question.

1. What does Pickles spend his time **learning** to do?

_____

_____

Analyzing the Literature

Provided below are discussion questions you can use in small groups, with the whole class, or for written assignments. Each question is written at two levels so you can choose the right question for each group of students. For each question, a few key points are provided for your reference as you discuss the book with students.

Story Element	Level 1	Level 2	Key Discussion Points
Setting	Where do the events in this chapter take place?	How has the setting changed in this chapter?	Prior to this, Pickles was living in a barrel and then temporarily in Mrs. Goodkind's home. The events in this chapter take place at the firehouse or fighting fires.
Plot	What does Mrs. Goodkind do at the start of this chapter?	How do we know that Mrs. Goodkind is still trying to help Pickles?	Mrs. Goodkind calls the fire chief and tells him that she thinks that Pickles isn't a bad cat and would probably like to live at the firehouse.
Character	What do we know about the fire chief?	Why doesn't the fire chief accept Pickles immediately?	The fire chief is a careful man. He says he won't accept Pickles until he proves he is a good firehouse cat. Then the fire chief watches Pickles's behavior before he decides to make him part of the fire team.
Character	What do Pickles's behaviors tell us?	What do we learn about Pickles's personality in this chapter?	In this chapter we learn that Pickles is a determined cat and a hard worker. He clearly wants to be a fire cat. He won't give up and keeps trying until he learns how to slide down the fire pole, ride in the fire truck, and help hold a hose.

Name _____ Date _____

Reader Response

Think

You have fire drills at school. They teach you how to leave the building if there is a fire. Close your eyes and remember the details of a fire drill.

Informative/Explanatory Writing Prompt

Describe what happened during a past fire drill. Make sure you tell everything in the order that it happened.

_____

_____

_____

_____

_____

_____

_____

_____

_____

Guided Close Reading

Closely reread the part about Pickles's meeting with the chief on page 48.

Directions: Think about these questions. In the space below, write ideas or draw pictures as you think. Be ready to share your answers.

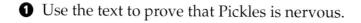

❶ Use the text to prove that Pickles is nervous.

❷ How does the punctuation in the text let you know that Pickles is surprised to see someone?

❸ Use the text to show how you know that Pickles realizes that something important is about to happen.

Name _____ Date _____

Making Connections–Then and Now

The Fire Cat was written more than 50 years ago. At that time, only men fought fires. Today women are firefighters, too. That is why we no longer call these community workers *firemen*.

Directions: Other things in the book are old fashioned, too. Answer these questions.

1. Look at the picture on page 33. How does the top of the desk look different than it might today?

   _____

   _____

   _____

   _____

2. Look at the picture on page 44. Describe how the fire truck looks different from a modern one.

   _____

   _____

   _____

   _____

3. Look at the picture on page 50. On another sheet of paper, draw what a modern team of firefighters would look like today.

Name _____ Date _____

Making Connections–Fire Safety

Directions: In this chapter, Pickles helps to fight a fire. If your clothes catch on fire, do not run! Read the captions. Draw pictures to show what you should do.

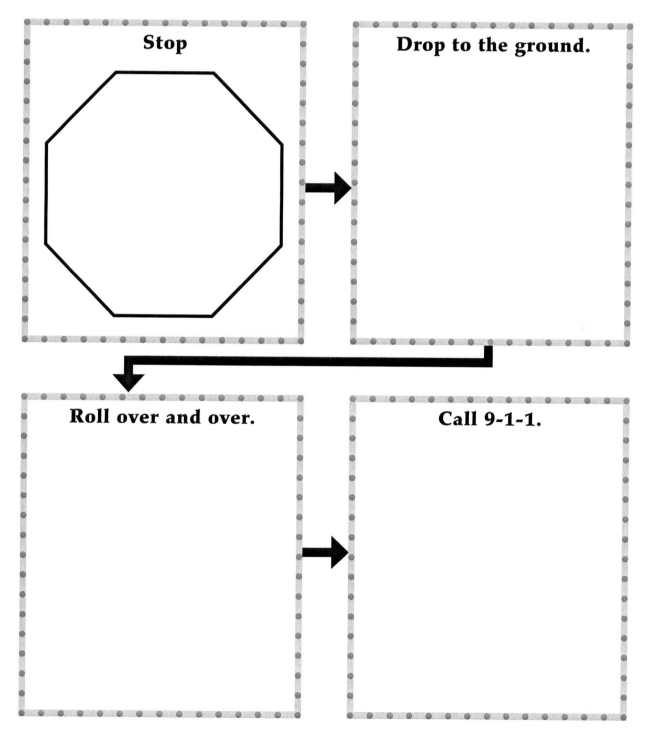

Stop

Drop to the ground.

Roll over and over.

Call 9-1-1.

Name _____ Date _____

Language Learning–Verbs

Directions: Read each word from the story. Write only the verbs inside the fire hat.

Language Hints!

- Verbs are action words.
- Verbs tell what is being done in a sentence.

Words from the Story

sitting	desk	telephone	rang
says	bell	send	ran
hear	fell	trucks	jump

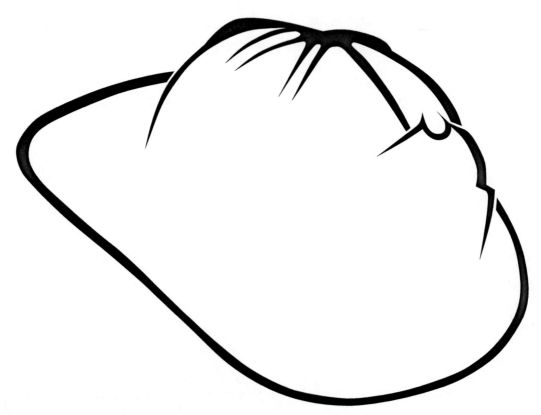

Story Elements-Setting

Directions: Study the book's illustrations of the firehouse (pages 32, 39, and 43). Then, draw the floor plan of the firehouse. A floor plan looks like you are looking down from the ceiling of the building.

Name _____ Date _____

Story Elements–Plot

Directions: The events in a story form its plot. Fill in the missing events from this story.

Joe brings Pickles to the firehouse.

↓

↓

Pickles works hard to become a good firehouse cat.

↓

↓

The chief, Mrs. Goodkind, and the whole fire team are gathered around the desk.

↓

Pre-Reading Picture Walk

1. Turn to page 3, which has the Table of Contents. Explain that this book has chapters. Ask students to identify the name of the third chapter and on what page it begins. *(The Old Tree; page 52)*

2. Turn to page 54. Cover the text. Have students describe what is happening in the picture. *(Pickles, wearing his fire hat, is sitting on the running board of the fire truck. Five other cats are on the truck, too.)* Predict what the picture means. *(Pickles is now getting along with other cats. The other cats look up to Pickles and want to be like him.)*

3. Turn to page 59. Ask, "Where is this happening?" *(It looks like the same tree where Pickles got stuck.)* "Why is Pickles the one going up the tree?" *(The cat is too high up for a man to reach.)*

4. Turn to pages 60 and 61. Ask, "What is Pickles doing?" *(He is rescuing the little cat. He is carrying the cat down the ladder by the scruff of its neck.)*

Vocabulary Overview

Key words and phrases from this section are provided below with definitions and sentences about how the words are used in the story. Introduce and discuss these important vocabulary words with students. If you think these words or other words in the story warrant more time devoted to them, there are suggestions in the introduction for other vocabulary activities (page 5).

Word	Definition	Sentence about Text
everyone (p. 53)	each person; all the people	The chief insists that Pickles be kind to **everyone**, including other cats.
rainy (p. 55)	having a lot of rain	On a **rainy** day, one of Mrs. Goodkind's cats gets stuck in a tree.
upstairs (p. 55)	on an upper floor of a building	Pickles likes to sit **upstairs** with the firefighters.
slid (p. 56)	moved smoothly; glided	The firefighters and Pickles **slide** down the pole.
gently (p. 61)	not hard or forceful	Pickles **gently** carries the cat down to Mrs. Goodkind.
beginning (p. 63)	the point or time at which something starts	Pickles knows that this is just the **beginning** of the big things he will do.
proud (p. 63)	feeling very happy and pleased because of something one has done	The fire cat is **proud** of himself.

Vocabulary Activity

Directions: Complete each sentence below. Use one of the words listed.

Words from the Story

rainy	upstairs	everyone	slid	gently	beginning

1. Pickles spends time _____ with the firefighters.

2. It is a cold, _____ day.

3. The firefighters _____ down the pole.

4. Pickles _____ carries the little cat down the ladder.

Directions: Answer this question.

5. Why does Pickles feel **proud**?

_____

_____

_____

_____

_____

_____

Analyzing the Literature

Provided below are discussion questions you can use in small groups, with the whole class, or for written assignments. Each question is written at two levels so you can choose the right question for each group of students. For each question, a few key points are provided for your reference as you discuss the book with students.

Story Element	Level 1	Level 2	Key Discussion Points
Character	What wise words does the fire chief tell Pickles?	How does the fire chief help Pickles to improve his personality?	The fire chief tells him that a fire cat must be kind to everyone. This makes Pickles stop chasing other cats and instead make friends with them for the first time in his life.
Setting	What does the weather remind you of?	Why is it significant that it is raining?	It is raining when Pickles rescues the cat from the tree, just like it was raining when Pickles was rescued from the same tree. The situation is identical—except that this time Pickles overcomes his fear.
Plot	How are the events in this chapter like the events in the first chapter?	Compare and contrast the events in the first chapter with this chapter.	In the first chapter, Pickles gets stuck in a tree and is rescued by firefighters. In this chapter, Pickles rescues another cat from the same tree because the firefighters can't reach the cat.
Character	How does Mrs. Goodkind feel at the end of the book?	Tell about Mrs. Goodkind's thoughts at the end of the book.	Mrs. Goodkind feels proud of Pickles. She is so glad she sent him to the firehouse with Joe because he has found his place in life and will get to do "big things" from now on.

Reader Response

Think

The little cat is stuck in a deciduous tree. This kind of tree has leaves and seeds. Coniferous trees have needles and cones. Which kind of tree do you prefer?

Opinion Writing Prompt

Do you like deciduous trees or coniferous trees better? Tell why. Include lots of details.

_____

_____

_____

_____

_____

_____

_____

_____

_____

Guided Close Reading

Closely reread the part about the frightened little cat on page 58.

Directions: Think about these questions. In the space below, write ideas or draw pictures as you think. Be ready to share your answers.

❶ What words in the story tell us that the firefighters are stumped about how to help the cat?

❷ Why is it significant that the cat needs to be rescued from this particular tree?

❸ Use the text to prove that Pickles is the only one who can save the little cat.

Making Connections-Carrying a Baby Mammal

Directions: On page 61, Pickles carries the little cat by the scruff of its neck. The scruff is a loose piece of skin on many mammals. It lets a mother carry a baby with her mouth. Look at the pictures. Circle the babies whose mothers carry them by the scruff.

Making Connections-Math Word Problems

Directions: Solve each math problem. Don't forget to label your answers!

1. Mrs. Goodkind calls the fire department for help at 5:00 p.m. The firefighters arrive at 5:25 p.m. How long does it take for them to get to the tree?

   _____

2. The ladder that Pickles climbs is 43 feet tall. The little cat is on a branch 65 feet above the ground. How many feet does Pickles have to climb from the top of the ladder to reach the cat?

   _____

3. Mrs. Goodkind has five cats. She adopts four new cats, but two of her original cats run away. How many cats does Mrs. Goodkind have in all?

   _____

4. Hook and Ladder Company 7 has a team of 17 firefighters. Three of them go with Pickles to rescue the cat in the tree. How many firefighters stay at the station?

   _____

Name _____ Date _____

Language Learning-Past Tense Verbs

Directions: Fill in the chart below. You can look through the chapter if you need to.

Language Hints!

- Often a *-d* or an *-ed* is added to the end of a verb to show the action happened in the past.

- Sometimes the whole word changes.

Verb	Past Tense Verb
call	*called*
hear	
love	
make	
say	
slide	
stand	
come	
climb	
ride	

Name _____ Date _____

Story Elements–Character

Directions: Think about Mrs. Goodkind. What do you know about her? Fill in the graphic organizer below with what you know about her from the story.

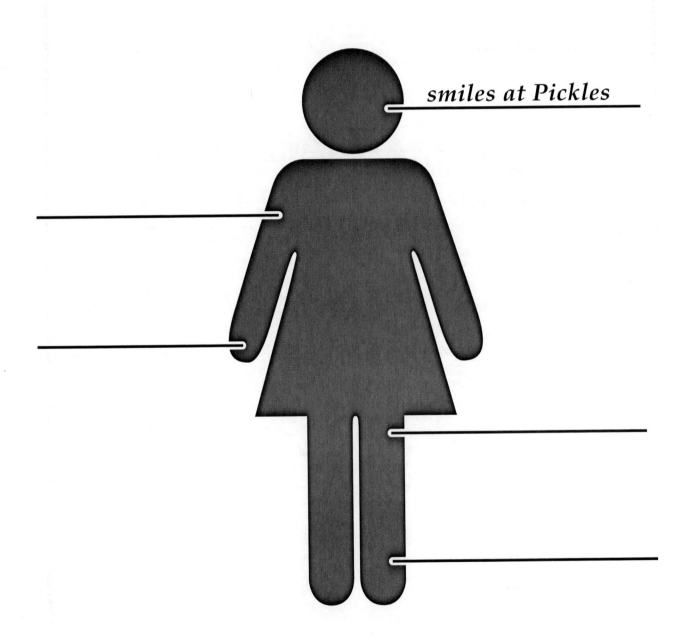

smiles at Pickles

Story Elements-Plot

Directions: Pretend you are Joe. Write a note to Pickles, telling him whether or not you are glad you brought him to the firehouse. Use events from the book to explain your feelings.

Dear Pickles,

_____

_____

_____

_____

_____

_____

_____

_____

_____

Your friend,

Joe

Name _____ Date _____

Post-Reading Theme Thoughts

Directions: Choose a main character from *The Fire Cat*. Pretend you are that character. Draw a picture of a happy face or a sad face to show how the character would feel about each statement. Then use words to explain your picture.

Character I Chose: _____

Statement	How Does the Character Feel? ☺ ☹	Why Does the Character Feel This Way?
I feel like I don't belong.		
I want to do something important.		
I work hard to show others I can do it.		
I like to help people in need.		

Culminating Activity:
Illustrate and Make a Book

Directions: Read the text on each page. Draw a picture to match. Then, cut out the pages. Put them in order and staple them together. Take your book home and read it to a family member.

The Fire Cat Saves the Day

Illustrated by _____

2

Pickles is a fire cat. He lives at the firehouse with the firefighters. His best friend is Joe. Pickles rides on the fire truck. He wears a special little fire hat.

Culminating Activity:
Illustrate and Make a Book (cont.)

3

One day Joe and the fire team rush to a house. Flames are coming out of the windows!

4

Pickles leaps out of the truck. He runs to the fire hydrant. He helps the firefighters to connect the hose.

Culminating Activity:
Illustrate and Make a Book (cont.)

5

Two firefighters aim the hose at the windows. They spray water on the flames. Two other firefighters enter the house. They look for people to save.

6

A firefighter comes out of the house. She carries a small boy. He is covered in ashes and looks sleepy. The firefighter lays the child on the ground. Pickles licks his cheek.

Culminating Activity:
Illustrate and Make a Book (cont.)

7

The boy's eyes fly open. He cries, "Snowball!" Then he sees
Pickles. "You are not Snowball! I want my cat!" the boy says.
He cries and cries.

Pickles realizes that Snowball is still inside the burning house!
Pickles runs into the fire.

8

The fire is hot. The flames crackle. The smoke fills Pickles's
lungs. He looks around. Where would a cat hide? He runs
behind the couch and sees a tiny white cat. Pickles grabs the cat
by the scruff of its neck. The cat is limp.

Culminating Activity:
Illustrate and Make a Book (cont.)

9

Pickles struggles to get out the door. He makes it outside and falls. Joe rushes over.

"Meow!" says Pickles.

10

"Meow!" Snowballs says weakly.

The little boy runs over. "Snowball!" he says and hugs the cat. "You saved my cat!"

Culminating Activity:
Illustrate and Make a Book *(cont.)*

11

The next week, the chief calls for Pickles. Pickles goes to his desk. The whole fire team is there.

12

So is the little boy whose house burned. He is holding Snowball.

Culminating Activity:
Illustrate and Make a Book (cont.)

13

The chief says, "Pickles, you do big things. You are a hero. You have earned a medal for bravery."

14

The medal is shiny. It is on a red ribbon. The chief ties the ribbon around Pickles's neck. "Long live our fire cat!" shouts the fire team.

Name _____ Date _____

Comprehension Assessment

Directions: Fill in the bubble for the best response to each question.

Section 1

1. What passage from the book proves that Pickles was bored?

(A) "Pickles' barrel was in an old yard where there was nothing big to do."

(B) "He chased the little cat out of the yard. It was a bad, bad thing."

(C) "He ran after little cats. It was all that Pickles could find to do."

(D) "One day Mrs. Goodkind said, 'Pickles, you are a mixed-up cat.'"

Section 2

2. What sentence shows that Pickles doesn't like being in the tree?

(E) "Pickles wanted to climb down. He wanted to get back into his barrel."

(F) "The fireman picked up Pickles and tucked him into his coat."

(G) "He could not climb down. Sometimes this happens to a cat."

(H) "Mrs. Goodkind ran to the firemen and pointed to Pickles."

Section 3

3. Why does Pickles worry that the chief won't let him stay in the firehouse?

_____

_____

Comprehension Assessment (cont.)

Section 3 (cont.)

4. What does Pickles receive as a reward for his efforts to learn how to be a firefighter?

(A) a visit from Mrs. Goodkind's cats

(B) a little fire hat

(C) a ride on the fire truck

(D) a phone call from the chief

Section 4

5. How does Pickles show courage?

(E) He learns how to climb a very tall ladder.

(F) He rescues a bird in the rain.

(G) He stops chasing other cats and welcomes them at the firehouse.

(H) He saves a cat from the same tree he had been afraid to climb down.

Name _____ Date _____

Response to Literature: Having a Pet

Having a pet is fun. It is also a lot of work. Pets need food, water, and love every day. They need to see a vet when they get sick. Having a pet can be sad when the pet dies.

Directions: Complete the word web below. In the circles, write reasons why having a pet is fun. In the squares, write reasons why having a pet is hard. Then answer the questions on the next page.

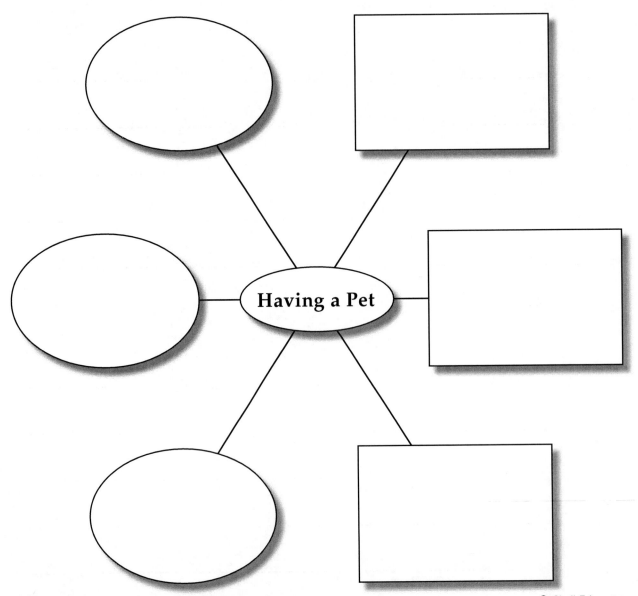

Response to Literature: Having a Pet (cont.)

1. What is the best reason for having a pet?

_____

_____

_____

_____

2. What is the hardest part about having a pet?

_____

_____

_____

_____

3. Why do you think the chief allows the firefighters to keep Pickles?

_____

_____

_____

_____

Name _____ Date _____

Response to Literature Rubric

Directions: Use this rubric to evaluate student responses.

Great Job	Good Work	Keep Trying
☐ You answered all three questions completely. You included many details.	☐ You answered all three questions.	☐ You did not answer all three questions.
☐ Your handwriting is very neat. There are no spelling errors.	☐ Your handwriting can be neater. There are some spelling errors.	☐ Your handwriting is not very neat. There are many spelling errors.
☐ Your graphic organizer is complete with at least six details.	☐ Your graphic organizer is mostly complete with at least four details.	☐ Your graphic organizer is not complete.
☐ Creativity is clear in both the graphic organizer and the writing.	☐ Creativity is clear in either the graphic organizer or the writing.	☐ There is not much creativity in the graphic organizer or the writing.

Teacher Comments: _____

_____

_____

_____

The responses provided here are just examples of what students may answer. Many accurate responses are possible for the questions throughout this unit.

Vocabulary Activity—Section 1:
Pickles (page 16)

- Each day Mrs. Goodkind gives Pickles **something** to eat.
- Pickles does not have **anything** useful to do.
- The empty **barrel** has **nothing** inside it.
- What will **happen** when a cat comes near Pickles?
- Pickles is both good and bad because he is a **mixed-up** cat.
1. The other cats run away, leaving Pickles lonely.

Guided Close Reading—Section 1:
Pickles (page 19)

1. "Every day Mrs. Goodkind gave Pickles something to eat." "She picked up the mixed-up cat. She took him into her home to live."
2. She said that Pickles is both a good cat and a bad cat.
3. This is an opinion question; allow for a variety of responses.

Language Learning—Section 1:
Pickles (page 22)

Adjectives to write in the frame: yellow, big, black, old, young, little, bad, and good

Story Elements—Section 1:
Pickles (page 23)

- **Pickles:** lives in a barrel, chases other cats, wants to do something big
- **Both:** fed by Mrs. Goodkind, cared about by Mrs. Goodkind
- **Mrs. Goodkind's Cats:** live in a nice house, say Pickles can't be their friend, have toys and furniture

Story Elements—Section 1:
Pickles (page 24)

These pictures should be circled: dog, garbage truck, city bus, and bottle marked *antifreeze*.

Vocabulary Activity—Section 2:
Pickles Up a Tree (page 27)

1. Mrs. Goodkind uses the telephone to call the fire department to save Pickles.

Guided Close Reading—Section 2:
Pickles Up a Tree (page 30)

1. "The wind began to blow. It blew and blew and blew. The rain came down hard. It came down harder and harder."
2. Pickles is mean to the little cat; he chases her up the tree and traps her there. However, when the weather gets terrible, he finally lets her leave.
3. "Pickles wanted to climb down. But he could not climb down."

Language Learning—Section 2:
Pickles Up a Tree (page 33)

- **Nouns:** rain, cat, barrel, ladder, tree, window, coat, fireman, wind
- **Proper nouns:** Pickles, Joe, Mrs. Goodkind

Story Elements—Section 2:
Pickles Up a Tree (page 35)

Five main events in order (allow for variation in wording):

- Pickles chases a little cat up a tree.
- At last, Pickles lets the little cat go.
- Pickles can't climb down the tree.
- Mrs. Goodkind calls the firefighters.
- Joe rescues Pickles and takes him back to the firehouse.

Vocabulary Activity—Section 3:
The Fire Cat (page 38)

1. Pickles spends his time learning to slide down the pole, ride on the truck, and help hold the hose.

Guided Close Reading—Section 3:
The Fire Cat (page 41)

1. "He said to himself, 'Maybe the Chief does not like the way I work. Maybe he wants to send me back to my old yard.'"
2. The author uses an exclamation point after Mrs. Goodkind to show that Pickles is surprised to see her at the firehouse.
3. "The next day the Chief called all the firemen to his desk. Then he called for Pickles. Pickles did not know what was going to happen."

Making Connections—Section 3:
The Fire Cat (page 42)

- The desk has an old rotary dial corded phone, and there is no computer screen or keyboard on the desk.

- You may need to show students a picture of a modern ladder fire truck for them to complete this question. The major difference is that today the firefighters ride inside an enclosed cab and the ladder does not detach from the truck—instead it is a turntable ladder that rises up several feet from the center of the truck and can reach many stories in height.

- The modern fire team drawing may include at least one woman and at least one ethnically diverse person.

Language Learning—Section 3:
The Fire Cat (page 44)

Verbs: sitting, says, hear, fell, send, rang, ran, jump

Story Elements—Section 3:
The Fire Cat (page 46)

The missing events in order: Mrs. Goodkind calls the chief and tells him Pickles wants to live in the firehouse; The firefighters praise Pickles, but the chief says nothing; and the chief gives Pickles his very own little fire hat.

Vocabulary Activity—Section 4:
The Old Tree (page 49)

1. Pickles spends time **upstairs** with the firefighters.
2. It is a cold, **rainy** day.
3. The firefighters **slid** down the pole.
4. Pickles **gently** carries the little cat down the ladder.
5. Pickles feels proud because he overcomes his fear and saves the little cat.

Guided Close Reading—Section 4:
The Old Tree (page 52)

1. "Joe said to Mrs. Goodkind, 'I don't know what to do.'"
2. It's significant because this is the same tree that Pickles was too afraid to climb down from.

3. "The little cat ran to a high branch, where a fireman could not go."

Making Connections—Section 4:
The Old Tree (page 53)

These pictures should be circled: a lion cub, a wolf cub, a polar bear cub, a tiger cub

Making Connections—Section 4:
The Old Tree (page 54)

1. 5:25 – 5:00 = 25 minutes
2. 65 – 43 = 22 feet
3. 5 + 4 – 2 = 7 cats
4. 17 – 3 = 14 firefighters

Language Learning—Section 4:
The Old Tree (page 55)

Past tense verbs: called, heard, loved, made, said, slid, stood, came, climbed, rode

Story Elements—Section 4:
The Old Tree (page 56)

What we know about Mrs. Goodkind: likes cats, is kind to Pickles when he's a mixed-up cat, calls the firehouse when cats are up a tree, encourages the chief to let Pickles be a fire cat, and praises Pickles for saving her cat.

Comprehension Assessment (pages 66–67)

1. C. "He ran after little cats. It was all that Pickles could find to do."
2. E. "Pickles wanted to climb down. He wanted to get back into his barrel."
3. The chief says Pickles can stay if he learns to be a good fire cat. The other firefighters praise Pickles three times, but the chief never says anything. So, when the chief calls Pickles to his desk, the cat is unsure what the chief will say.
4. B. a little fire hat
5. H. He saves a cat from the same tree he had been afraid to climb down.